Flowers in Love 4

Flowers in Love 4

Moniek Vanden Berghe

Photography
Kurt Dekeyzer
Kris Dimitriadis

stichting
kunstboek

Bridal bouquets – to this day they still evoke the greatest amount of passion among floral arrangers. Most floral designers are also keen followers of the world of fashion, an ever-changing art form that constantly spurs itself to create, innovate and develop. To some degree floristry remains a 'service' art form, one in which artists must adhere to the specific requests and wishes of their customers. But there is always room for creativity when it comes to creating a striking and heartfelt work. And it is precisely in that artistic space – no matter how small it may sometimes be – that florists are able to stand out from the bunch. Our job is to use our creative input to reflect the bride's personality and highlight the beauty of her dress.

This fresh edition of Flowers in Love is thanks entirely to my fellow florists, both professionals and trainees. Their undying enthusiasm remains a major incentive and always inspires me afresh to seek out challenging designs and new approaches to bridal floristry. In Flowers in Love 4 I go in search of original methods and techniques for taking the basic materials that can be found anywhere (such as salal, bear grass, aspidistra, or cork) and transforming them. This makes the ideas presented in this book universal in nature and they can be used everywhere and by anyone. Going a step further, I like to use local and personal materials – favourites plucked from the garden or the wilds – as special, distinguishing, evocative or fragile accents.

Creating the right combinations and ratios remains the very essence of floral design. Crafting the perfect bouquet for a perfect bride, uncovering the right design for a specific dress, or creating a fitting floral atmosphere for that unique couple. To combine flowers with other plant materials, balance textures, structures and forms, eliminate the superfluous and retain the essence, to simplify where possible and enrich where necessary – all these aspects and more are what I love most about my art.

Bridal bouquets must of course also be wearable. Volume, dimensions, weight consequently remain important criteria in my designs. Furthermore, a bridal bouquet must always be surprising – a design that the bride and her entourage will never tire of.

Of course Flowers in Love 4 contains a great deal more than bridal bouquets alone. The associated bridal floristry in all its colourful diversity is given extensive space. This includes inspiring church decorations, car/carriage adornments, corsages, hairpieces, flower arrangements for bridesmaids, floral table decorations for the bridal table or buffet table and much more – all those small and distinctive details that make this special day even more unique and unforgettable.

Moniek Vanden Berghe

First of all Moniek is a treasured friend and soulmate. We love to explore and discover beautiful gardens together. Gardens are places where our passion for flowers, plants, architecture and design comes to life. I take my hat off to Moniek and never cease to be amazed by her extraordinary craftsmanship. She started out her career in a different trade, but her innate feel for colours and shapes developed into a very personal floral design style that is inspiring to colleagues all over the world.
Geert Pattyn, Geluwe, Belgium

I have always been enthralled by Moniek Vanden Berghe's work. I have had the pleasure to visit her studio to see in person, the incredible craftsmanship that is evident in each and every composition she has created.
Flowers in Love 4 has within its volume, a beautifully crafted collection of bridal designs showcasing her latest techniques. As in every volume of the Flowers in Love series, Moniek creatively combines her stylistic constructions with exquisite textural sensitivity and a delicious color palette.
This new book will provide unseen ideas to a new generation of brides, and will inspire floral professionals worldwide.
Hitomi Gilliam AIFD, Vancouver, Canada

While it is often noted that beauty is in the eye of the beholder, in the case of Moniek Vanden Berghe beauty is not only in her eyes but also in her hands, her mind and, most importantly, her heart. Flowers in Love 4 continues to demonstrate Moniek's unrivaled sensitivity to flowers and plant materials and the imaginative thinking she brings to the world of bridal floristry. Her intuitive ability to balance form and function while retaining the soul of the design ingredients, and to reference the occasion and the bride's unique qualities is a gift – a gift shared generously with everyone fortunate enough to read this new volume.
Mark Pampling, Alstonville, Australia

Moniek continues to uphold her reputation as one of the world's most influential floral designers. Renowned for her contemporary yet romantic approach, her bridal work has become synonymous with originality and femininity. With the publication of Flowers in Love 4, yet again Moniek inspires us through her love of flowers and nature together with her innate sense of style.
Neill Strain, Neill Strain Floral Couture, Londen, UK

I feel very fortunate that I have come across people in life who never cease to inspire me. Looking at you, I have come to realize that there are things which are difficult to put into words, but which you can so beautifully express in arts, where colors, fabrics and form come together so perfectly. It's the kind of art that awakens feelings and fills one's heart with emotions. Thank you for the talent and inspiration that you give to each one of us.
Vadim Kazanskiy, Novosibirsk, Russia

Endless sweetness and the urge to reveal and translate life's essences by means of lines, shapes and colours into a beautiful tale of flowers, that's Moniek in a nutshell.
Rudy Casati, Milan, Italy

Les bouquets de mariée suscitent aujourd'hui encore la passion la plus totale parmi les décorateurs floraux. La plupart des créateurs suivent avec enthousiasme le monde de la mode, un art en perpétuelle transformation stimulé par la création, l'innovation et le développement. D'une certaine manière, la décoration florale reste un art proposé sous forme de « service », dans lequel les artistes doivent adhérer aux demandes et souhaits spécifiques de leurs clients. Mais la créativité trouve toujours sa place lorsqu'il s'agit de construire une œuvre saisissante et sincère. C'est précisément dans cet espace artistique, quelle qu'en soit la taille, que les fleuristes ont l'opportunité de se démarquer. Notre rôle est de mettre en application notre créativité afin d'illustrer la personnalité de la mariée et de souligner la beauté de sa robe.

Cette nouvelle édition de Flowers in Love doit sa naissance à mes camarades fleuristes, professionnels et en formation. Leur enthousiasme éternel reste un encouragement qui m'inspire à relever les défis en proposant de nouvelles approches créatives dans mes compositions florales. Dans Flowers in Love 4, j'explore des méthodes et techniques originales basées sur les matériaux de base qu'offre la nature (comme le salal, l'herbe d'ours, l'aspidistra ou le liège) afin de les transformer. Grâce à cette démarche, les idées présentées dans cet ouvrage deviennent universelles et peuvent être récupérées dans la nature par tout un chacun. Afin d'aller plus loin, j'aime utiliser les matériaux locaux et personnels, cueillis directement dans mon jardin ou dans la nature, pour en faire des notes spéciales, distinctives, évocatrices ou fragiles.

Obtenir les bonnes combinaisons en respectant l'harmonie constitue l'essence de la décoration florale. Il s'agit de créer le bouquet parfait pour une mariée parfaite, proposer un modèle approprié à une robe spécifique, ou créer une atmosphère florale adaptée à chaque couple. Combiner les fleurs avec d'autres plantes, harmoniser les textures, les structures et les formes, éliminer le superflu pour conserver l'essence, simplifier et enrichir si nécessaire : tous ces aspects, parmi tant d'autres, représentent ce que j'aime le plus dans cette forme d'expression artistique.

Les bouquets de mariée se doivent aussi d'être pratiques, et le volume, les dimensions, le poids et la cohérence restent des critères essentiels dans mes créations. De plus, un bouquet de mariée doit toujours être surprenant : un modèle dont la mariée et son entourage ne se lasseront jamais.

Bien sûr, Flowers in Love 4 contient bien plus que des bouquets de mariée et fait la part belle aux compositions florales dans toute leur diversité de couleurs. On y retrouve des décorations d'église inspirantes, des parures de voiture et de calèche, des corsages, des coiffes, des arrangements floraux pour les demoiselles d'honneur, des décorations destinées à la table de la mariée ou du buffet, et bien plus encore. Ce sont ces petits détails distincts qui rendront encore plus unique ce jour déjà très spécial.

Moniek Vanden Berghe

Moniek est tout d'abord une très grande amie. J'adore découvrir de beaux jardins en sa compagnie. C'est là que je ressens le mieux l'affinité que nous partageons pour les fleurs et les plantes, mais également pour l'architecture et le design.
Coup de chapeau pour son extraordinaire métier. Elle n'est pas née dans les fleurs mais cela ne l'a pas empêchée d'avoir développé un style très personnel qui inspire ses collègues dans les quatre coins du monde.
Geert Pattyn, Geluwe, Belgique

J'ai toujours été captivée par le travail de Moniek Vanden Berghe. J'ai eu la chance de visiter son studio et de voir de mes propres yeux le savoir-faire incroyable qui est évident dans chacune de ses compositions.
Flowers in Love 4 rassemble en son volume une magnifique collection de bouquets de mariée mettant en scène ses dernières techniques. Comme dans chaque volume de la série Flowers in Love, Moniek allie de manière créative ses constructions stylistiques, son incroyable sensibilité en matière de texture et une délicieuse palette de couleurs. Ce nouvel ouvrage proposera des idées inédites à une nouvelle génération de mariées et inspirera les fleuristes professionnels du monde entier.
Hitomi Gilliam AIFD, Vancouver, Canada

On entend souvent que la beauté naît du regard de celui qui la contemple, mais dans le cas de Moniek Vanden Berghe, la beauté n'est pas seulement dans ses yeux mais aussi dans ses mains, son esprit et, surtout, dans son cœur.
Flowers in Love 4 continue de démontrer la sensibilité sans égale de Moniek pour les fleurs et les plantes, ainsi que la pensée imaginaire qu'elle apporte au monde de la décoration florale destinée aux mariées. Sa capacité intuitive à harmoniser la forme et la fonctionnalité, à conserver l'âme de ses conceptions, à exprimer l'importance de l'occasion et les qualités uniques de la mariée est un don qu'elle partage généreusement avec tous les lecteurs de ce nouveau volume.
Mark Pampling, Alstonville, Australia

Moniek maintient sa réputation de créatrice florale parmi les plus influentes au monde. Connue pour son approche à la fois contemporaine et romantique, son travail auprès des mariées est devenu synonyme d'originalité et de féminité.
Avec la publication de Flowers in Love 4, Moniek nous inspire à nouveau à travers son amour des fleurs et de la nature, ainsi que par son sens inné du style.
Neill Strain, Neill Strain Floral Couture, Londres, Royaume-Uni

J'ai la chance d'avoir rencontré des personnes qui ne cessent de m'inspirer. J'ai réalisé grâce à elles que si parfois les mots viennent à manquer, certaines choses s'expriment merveilleusement à travers l'art, où les couleurs, les matières et les formes s'unissent dans la beauté. Ces œuvres nous révèlent des sentiments et remplissent notre cœur d'émotions. Merci pour le talent et l'inspiration que vous offrez à chacun d'entre nous.
Vadim Kazanskiy, Novosibirsk, Rusland

Une amabilité hors pair et le désir de dévoiler et de traduire la quintessence de la vie par des lignes, des formes et des couleurs dans une histoire de fleurs, voilà ce que représente Moniek pour moi.
Rudy Casati, Milan, Italie

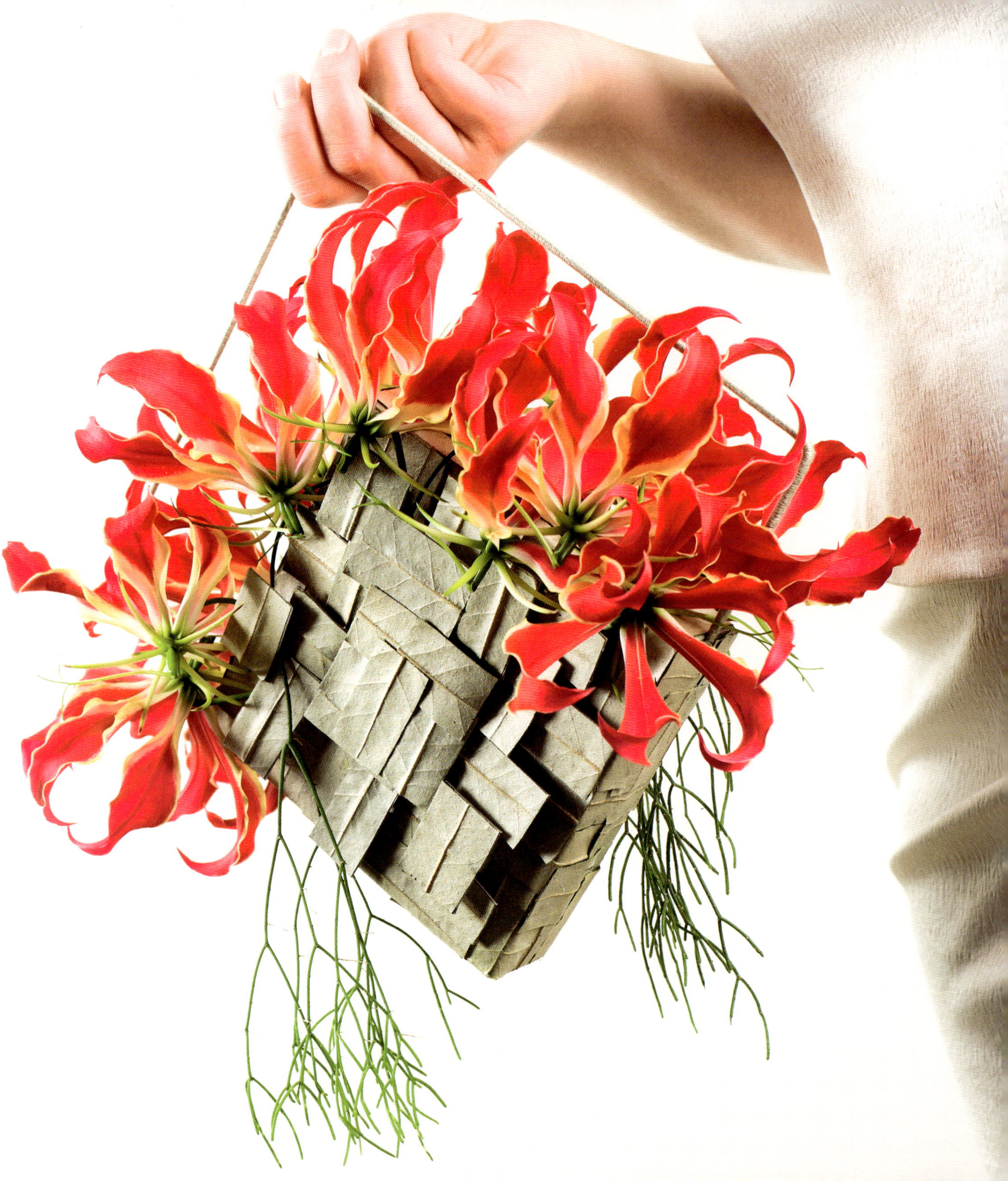

Bruidsboeketten, ze blijven de grote passie van bloemsierkunstenaars. De meeste floral designers houden ook van mode, een kunst die nooit stilstaat en voortdurend blijft prikkelen om zelf te creëren, te innoveren en te evolueren. Floristiek blijft voor een stuk een 'dienende' kunst, waarin artiesten zich moeten schikken naar de specifieke wensen en verlangens van opdrachtgevers.

Toch blijft altijd ruimte voor creativiteit bij het ontwerpen van een sprekende, doorvoelde creatie. Het is net in die artistieke manoeuvreerruimte, hoe klein soms ook, dat floristen zich kunnen onderscheiden. Het is onze taak om dankzij onze creatieve inzet de persoonlijkheid van de bruid te weerspiegelen en de schoonheid van de jurk te benadrukken.

Deze nieuwe Flowers in Love kwam er dankzij collega's en cursisten-floristen. Hun nooit aflatende enthousiasme blijft een grote stimulans en steekt me steeds opnieuw aan om te zoeken naar uitdagende vormen en nieuwe benaderingen van bruidswerk.

In Flowers in Love 4 zoek ik naar originele manieren en technieken om basismaterialen die overal te vinden zijn (zoals salal, beregras, Aspidistra, kurk,...) te verwerken. Zo worden de aangereikte ideeën universeel en kunnen ze overal en door iedereen toegepast worden. Daarnaast gebruik ik als bijzonder, onderscheidend, sprekend of fragiel accent graag heel lokale, persoonlijke materialen, favorieten uit de tuin of de natuur.

In bloemsierkunst blijft het vinden van juiste combinaties en verhoudingen de essentie. Het maken van het perfecte boeket voor deze bruid, het vinden van de juiste vormgeving voor deze specifieke jurk, het scheppen van een passende florale sfeer voor dit unieke koppel. Het combineren van bloemen en andere vegetatieve materialen, het uitbalanceren van texturen, structuren en vormen, het elimineren van wat overbodig is en het behouden van de essentie, vereenvoudigen waar mogelijk, verrijken waar nodig... dat blijft mijn meest geliefde aspect van dit mooie werk.

Bruidsboeketten moeten ook draagbaar zijn. Volume, dimensie, gewicht en hanteerbaarheid zijn daarom altijd belangrijke criteria in mijn ontwerpen. Verder moet een bruidsboeket ook altijd verrassend zijn en mag een bruid en haar entourage er niet op uitgekeken geraken.

Flowers in Love 4 bevat uiteraard nog veel meer dan bruidsboeketten. Ook het bijhorende bruidsbloemwerk in al zijn kleurige diversiteit komt ruim aan bod: inspirerende kerkversieringen, wagendecoraties, corsages, haarstukjes bloemen voor de bruidskindjes, florale aankleding van de feesttafel of het buffet,... al die kleine onderscheidende details die de grote dag uniek en bijzonder maken.

Moniek Vanden Berghe

Moniek is eerst en vooral een fijne vriendin. Samen mooie tuinen ontdekken is fantastisch. Onze zielsverwantschap voor bloemen, planten, architectuur en design komt er tot leven. Maar ook hoedje af voor haar vakmanschap. Ze werd niet direct in de bloemen geboren, maar met haar gevoel voor vorm en kleur ontwikkelde ze een heel persoonlijke stijl die inspirerend is voor collega's over de hele wereld.
Geert Pattyn, Geluwe, België

Het werk van Moniek Vanden Berghe blijft boeien. Ik had het grote genoegen om haar studio te bezoeken en met eigen ogen het ongelofelijke vakmanschap te zien waarmee zij elk van haar composities vormgeeft.
Flowers in Love 4 bevat een prachtige collectie bruidsboeketten waarin Moniek haar nieuwste technieken demonstreert. Zoals elk volume van de reeks Flowers in Love combineert Moniek op een creatieve manier haar stilistische composities met een opmerkelijk gevoel voor textuur en een heerlijk kleurenpallet.
Dit nieuwe boek zal een grote inspiratiebron zijn voor een nieuwe generatie bruiden en professionele floristen wereldwijd.
Hitomi Gilliam AIFD, Vancouver, Canada

Er wordt vaak gezegd dat schoonheid iets is dat zich afspeelt in de ogen van de toeschouwer, maar in het geval van Moniek Vanden Berghe zit schoonheid niet alleen in haar ogen maar ook in haar handen, geest en vooral in haar hart. Flowers in Love 4 is een vervolg op het prachtige verhaal van Monieks grote gevoeligheid voor bloemen en planten en de creativiteit waarmee zij de wereld van de bloemsierkunst en meer bepaald van de bruidsboeketten injecteert. Zij slaagt er op haar intuïtieve manier in om vorm en functionaliteit in balans te brengen, om de ziel van de gebruikte materialen te bewaren in haar ontwerpen, en om het belang van de gelegenheid en de kwaliteiten van de bruid in de verf te zetten. Een gave die zij in deze nieuwe uitgave op genereuze manier deelt met haar lezers.
Mark Pampling, Alstonville, Australia

Moniek bevestigt haar reputatie van een van de invloedrijkste floristen ter wereld te zijn. Ze wordt gewaardeerd voor haar hedendaagse en romantische stijl. Haar werk staat voor originaliteit en vrouwelijkheid. Met Flowers in Love 4 inspireert Moniek ons opnieuw met haar liefde voor bloemen en natuur, maar evenzeer met haar aangeboren zin voor stijl.
Neill Strain, Neill Strain Floral Couture, Londen, UK

Ik heb het grote geluk om mensen te ontmoeten die mij blijven inspireren. Ontmoetingen die mij doen inzien dat, waar woorden tekortschieten, er nog altijd de kunst is, met haar kleuren, materialen en vormen die zo'n mooi geheel vormen. Kunst die gevoelens oproept en ons hart vervult met emotie. Mijn oprechte dank voor jouw talent en inspiratie.
Vadim Kazanskiy, Novosibirsk, Rusland

Een eindeloos groot hart en het verlangen om de essentie van het leven te delen en te vertalen in een fascinerend verhaal van lijnen, vormen en bloemen. Dat is Moniek in een notendop.
Rudy Casati, Milaan, Italië

Eleagnus
Kalanchoë 'Paris'
Rosa sp.
Rubus tricolor

Raffia
Rosa 'Bombastic'
shells

Morus
Rosa 'Pink Piano'

Cortina
Tulipa (French double tulip)

Alstroemeria 'Nadya'
Fargesia (bamboo knot cocktail picks)

Eleagnus
Germini 'Pomponi Black Pearl'
Rosa 'Cappuccino'
Rosa 'Kahala'

Briza maxima
Eleagnus
Fritillaria meleagris
Helleborus
Rosa 'Cappuccino'
Scabiosa
wool

Calamus rotang
Clematis armandii
Dendrobium 'Nobile'

Calamus rotang
Ranunculus
Vanda Tayanee® 'White'
Xerophyllum tenax

Agapanthus
Anemone blanda 'Blue shades'
Calamus rotang
Hydrangea macrophylla 'Pimpernel'
Ozothamnus
Rhipsalis
Rosa 'Blanchette'
Viburnum opulus
Viola
paper

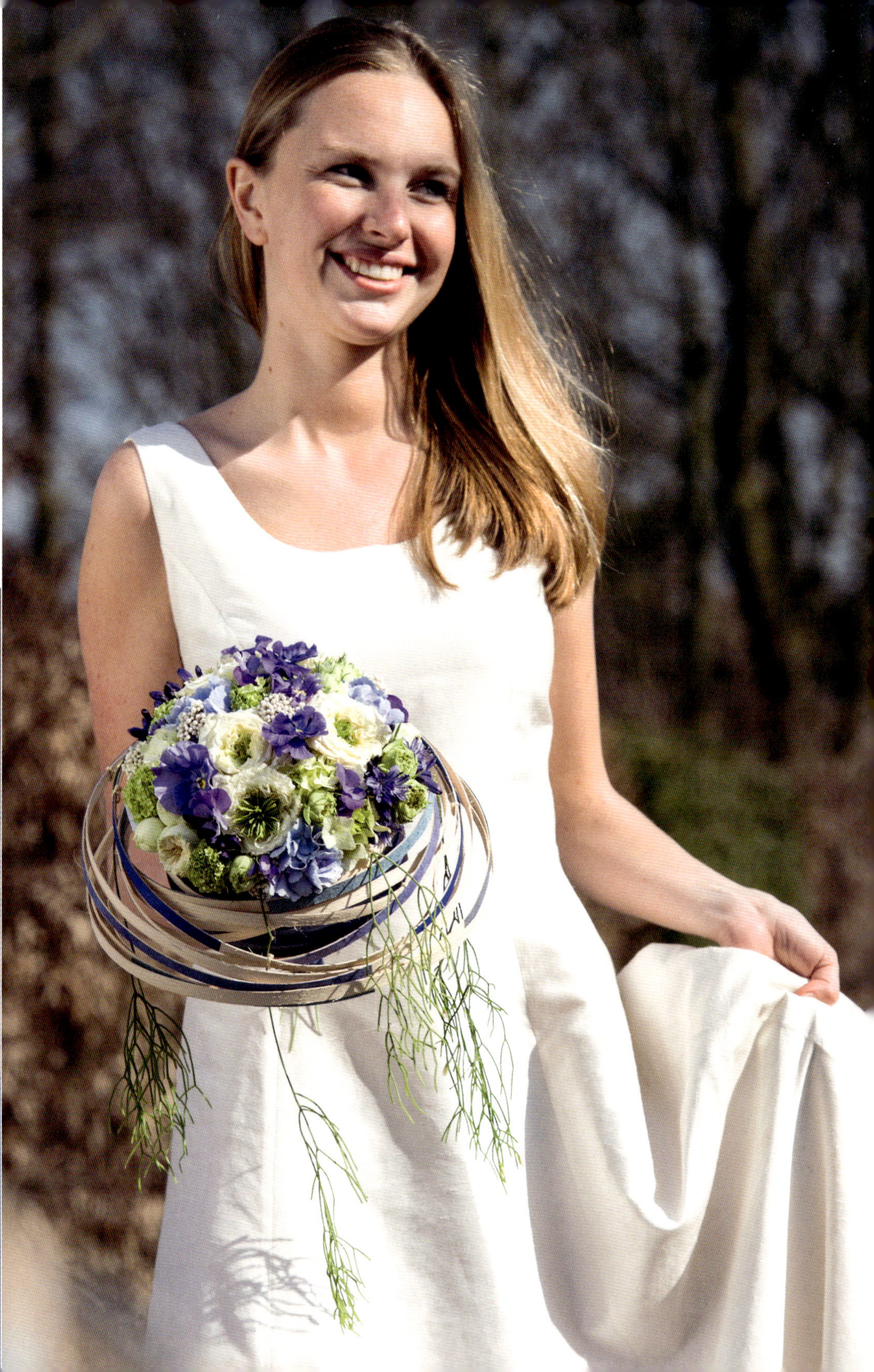

Agapanthus
Anemone blanda 'Blue Shades'
Calamus rotang
Dianthus barbatus 'Green Trick'
Helleborus
Hydrangea macrophylla 'Pimpernel'
Ozothamnus
Rosa 'Blanchette'
Viburnum opulus
Viola
paper

Dianthus Raffine® 'Elea'
Helleborus
Rosa 'Blanchette'
Rosa 'Dolcetta'
Senecio rowleyanus

Cordyline fruticosa 'Black Tie'
Dianthus Raffine® 'Elea'
Fritillaria meleagris
paper

Cortina
Ozothamnus
Ranunculus
Rosa 'Bombastic'

Dianthus Raffine® 'Elea'
Fritillaria meleagris
Ozothamnus
Ranunculus
Rosa 'Bombastic'

Capsella bursa-pastoris
Eleagnus
Phalaenopsis

Clematis tangutica
Colmanara 'Massai Red'
Peperomia
Rosa 'Bombastic'
Viburnum opulus

Cortina
Hypericum
Rosa 'Blanchette'
Rosa 'Latin Pompon'

Calistegia sepium
Dianthus barbatus 'Green Trick'
Fuchsia dependens 'Sunset Fuchsia'
Lunaria annua
Rosa 'Bombastic'
Rosa 'Moniek Vanden Berghe'
Rubus tricolor
Sanguisorba

Rosa
(Avalane stabilized rose)

Agapanthus
Dianthus
Eleagnus
Rosa 'Grand Prix'
Rosa 'Mirabel'
Vanda Tayanee® 'Blue'

Rosa
(Avalane stabilized rose)

Allium vineale
Vanda Sunanda® 'Lava'
Vanda Sunanda® 'Moonlight Blue'
Vanda Natcha® 'Tangelo'
veneer

Dendrobium nobile
Raffia

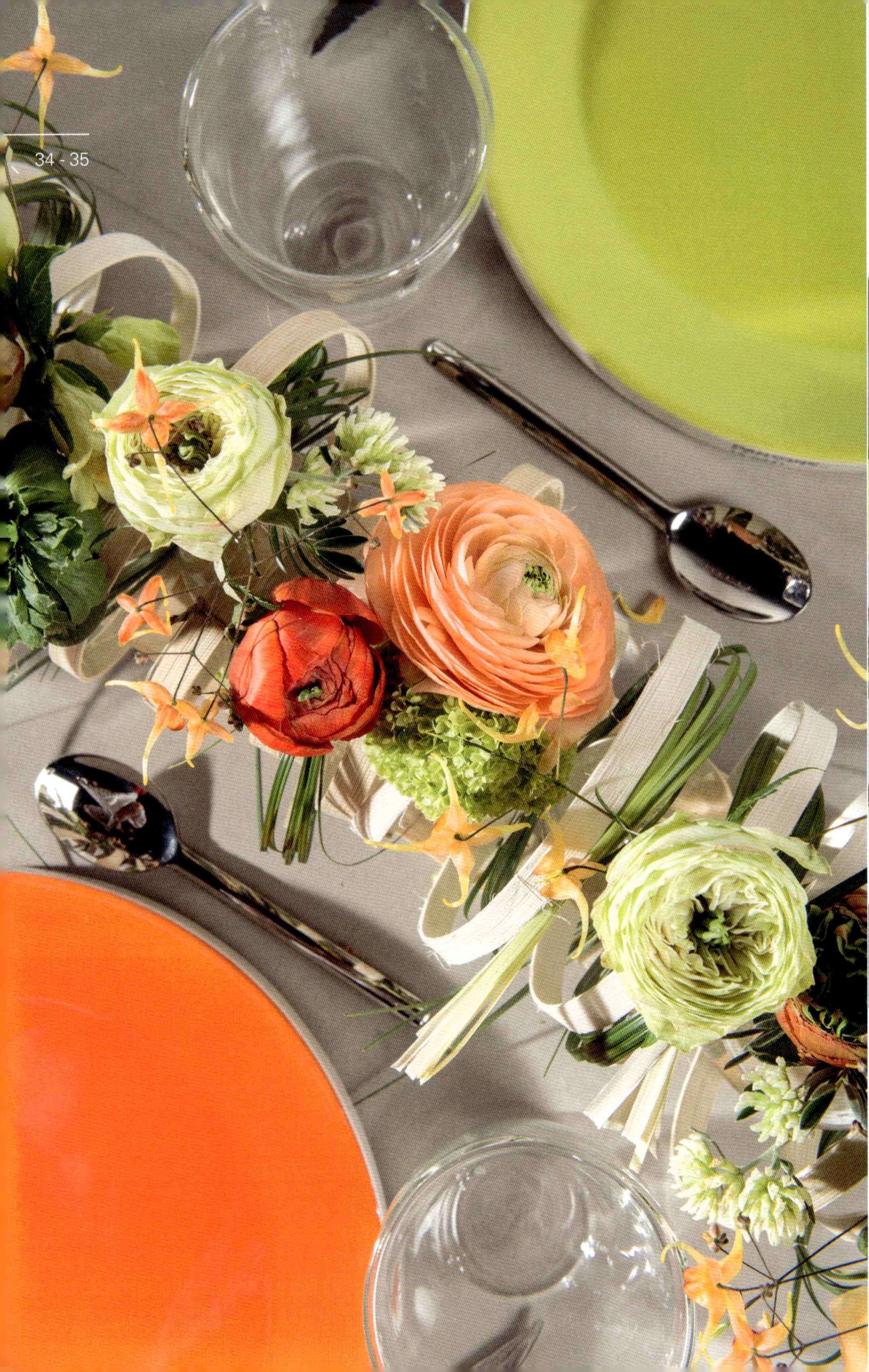

PANTONE
UNIVERSE
16-1260

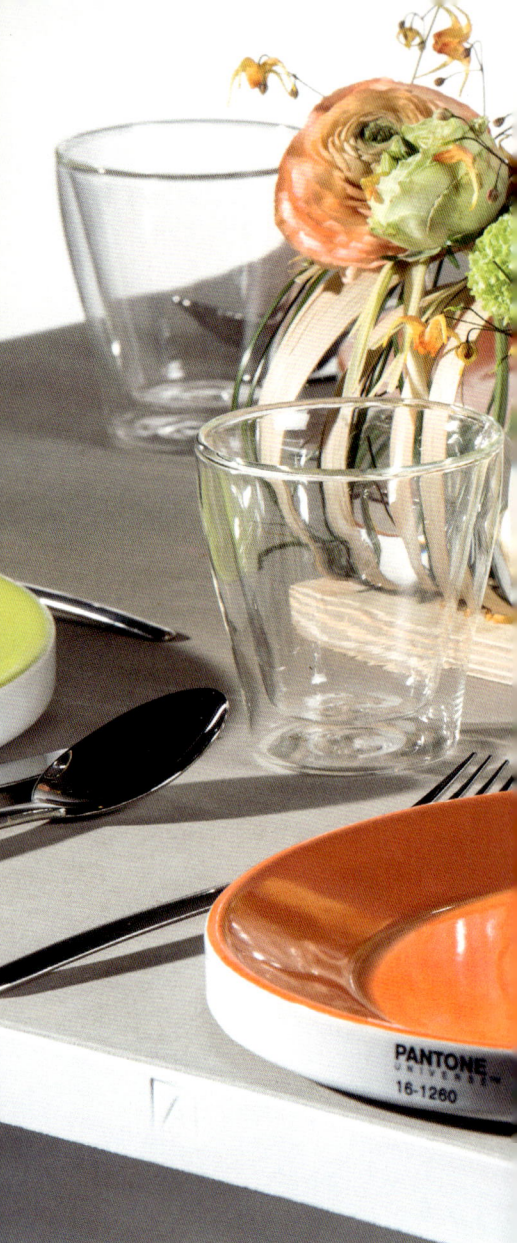

Epimedium
Ranunculus
Rosa 'Cappuccino'
Rosa 'Latin Pompon'
Trifolium campestre
Viburnum opulus
veneer

Cortina
Hyacinthus orientalis
Senecio rowleyanus
Vanda Natcha® 'Mandarin'
Vanda Natcha® 'Tangelo'

Cortina
Hyacinthus orientalis
Vanda Natcha® 'Orange'
Vanda Natcha®'Mandarin'

Hyacinthus orientalis
Vanda Natcha® 'Mandarin'
Vanda Natcha® 'Tangelo'
paper lantern

Alnus
Gypsophilla
Ozothamnus
Ranunculus
Skimmia japonica
Vanda Natcha® 'Honey Drops'
Vanda Natcha® 'Tangelo'

Calamus rotang
Prunus laurocerasus
Vanda Natcha® 'Mandarin'
Vanda Natcha® 'Tangelo'
paper

Cortina
Craspedia globosa
Lisianthus 'Rosita White'
Matricaria eximia
Vanda Nitaya® 'Magic Lemon'

Calamus rotang
Dianthus barbatus 'Green Trick'
Eucharis
Ranunculus
veneer

Anthriscus sylvestris
Dianthus barbatus 'Green Trick'
Rosa 'Green Eye'

Dendrobium nobile
Kalanchoë 'Paris'

Calamus rotang
Dianthus 'Apple Blossom'
Fritillaria meleagris
Helleborus
Ranunculus
Xerophyllum tenax

Calamus rotang
Fritillaria meleagris
Hoya linearis
Phalaenopsis 'Montecarlo'
Ranunculus (green and aubergine)
Vanda Divana® 'Pink and Mahogany'

Akebia quinata
Aspidistra
Fritillaria
Helleborus
Iberis sempervirens
paper
wood and wooden skewers

Dianthus barbatus 'Green Trick'
Dianthus 'Moon Aqua'
Gaultheria shallon
Oxalis debilis
Ranunculus
Vanda Tayanee® 'White'

Clematis 'Multi Blue'
Eleagnus
Vanda Tayanee® 'Blue'
Vicia cracca

Hydrangea
Phalaenopsis 'Kolibri Belize'

Nigella damascena
Rosa 'Milky Moments'
cork

Bromus sterilis
Calystegia sepium
Morus
Nigella damascena
Ribes rubrum
Rosa 'Milky Moments'

Rosa 'Blue Pacific'
Rosa 'Ocean Song'
Rosa 'Vendela'
Vanda 'Champagne'
ribbon

Hyacinthus orientalis
Pandanus
Phalaenopsis 'Kolibri Belize'
Vanda Sunanda® 'Chocolate Brown'

Dianthus Raffine® 'Elea'
Eleagnus
Helleborus
Rosa 'Blanchette'
Rosa 'Dolcetta'

Anemone pulsatilla
Clematis
Cortina
Geranium sp.
Rosa sp.
Scabiosa
Viburnum opulus

Calystegia sepium
Dendrobium nobile
Lunaria annua
Vanda Tayanee® 'White'
wool

Dianthus barbatus 'Green Trick'
Fritillaria meleagris
Gaultheria shallon
Ranunculus 'Pon Pon'
Ranunculus (white)
Senecio rowleyanus
paper

Chasmantium
Clematis tangutica
Dahlia hybride
Eleagnus
Rosa 'Blanchette'
Spirea
Typha latifolia

Bellis perennis
Calendula
Cordyline 'Black Tie'
Narcissus
Rosa sp.
Salix

Helianthus annuus 'Sonja'
Nigella
Sandersonia
Sanguisorba
Vanda

Lathyrus odoratus
Typha latifolia

Fargesia
Gautheria shallon
Hyacinthus orientalis
Raffia
Vanda Tayanee® 'White'

Gaultheria shallon
Hyacinthus orientalis
Zantedeschia 'Captain
Venture'

Azalea Hortinno®
Noralinde® 'Belli'

Amsonia orientalis
Clematis 'Blue Pirouette'
Delphinium hybr.
Passiflora
Vicia cracca
paper

Buxus
Hydrangea macrophylla 'Pimpernel'
Ranunculus
Vanda Tayanee® 'White'

Myosotis
Senecio hybridus
Senecio rowleyanus
Viola
Xanthorrhoea

Lunaria annua
Nigella damascena

Fargesia
Senecio rowleyanus
Zantedeschia 'Captain Venture'
shells

Briza maxima
Pandanus
Rosa 'Blanchette'
Skimmia japonica
Vanda Sunanda® 'Deep Chocolate Brown'
veneer

Astrantia
Bromus sterilis
Clematis 'Climbing Star'
Cotinus coggygria
Phlebodium
Rosa 'Mentha'
ribbon and rope

Cortina
Ranunculus
wool

Phalaenopsis
'Kolibri Brazil'
Phalaenopsis 'Montecarlo'
cork

Anemone pulsatilla
Asclepias 'Moby Dick'
Clematis tangutica
Eleagnus
Rosa 'Snowflake'
Viburnum opulus
Zantedeschia 'Captain Venture'
seedpods

Alchemilla mollis
Castanea
Paeonia 'Duchesse de Nemours'
Ribes rubrum

Chrysanthemum 'Santini'
Zantedeschia 'Captain Venture'

Lathyrus
Zantedeschia 'Captain Venture'

Begonia
Cortina
Rubus tricolor

Carex
Hypericum 'Cream Classic'
Leymus arenaris
Nigella damascena
Osteospermum 'Summertime Sweet Red Velvet'
Surfinia
Rosa 'Blanchette'
Rubus tricolor
Triticum

Agapanthus
Gaultheria shallon
Ranunculus
Spirea japonica 'Bridal Veil'

Aspidistra
Betula
Spirea japonia 'Bridal Veil'
Xerophyllum tenax
Zantedeschia 'Captain Venture'

Anthurium
Clematis tangutica
Kalanchoë 'Paris'
Lathyrus odoratus
Rosa 'Blanchette'
Typha latifolia

Anthurium
Kalanchoë 'Paris'

Anthurium
Clematis tangutica
Kalanchoë 'Paris'

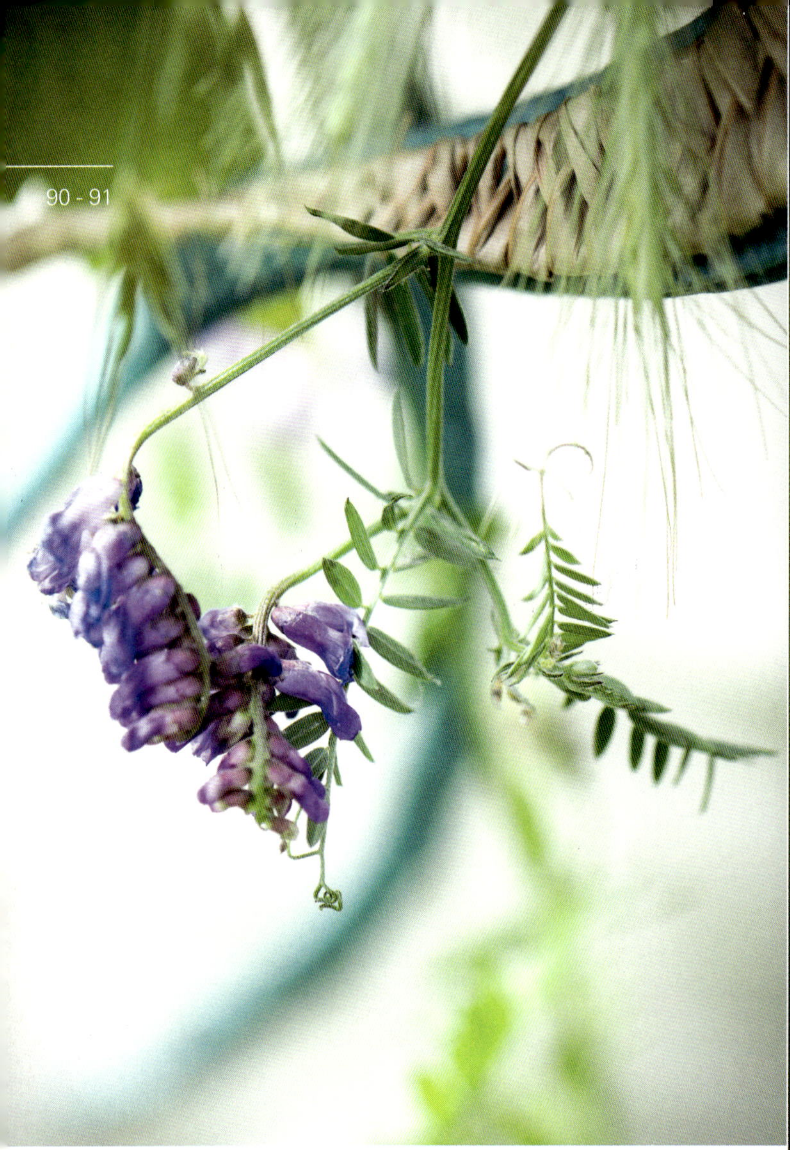

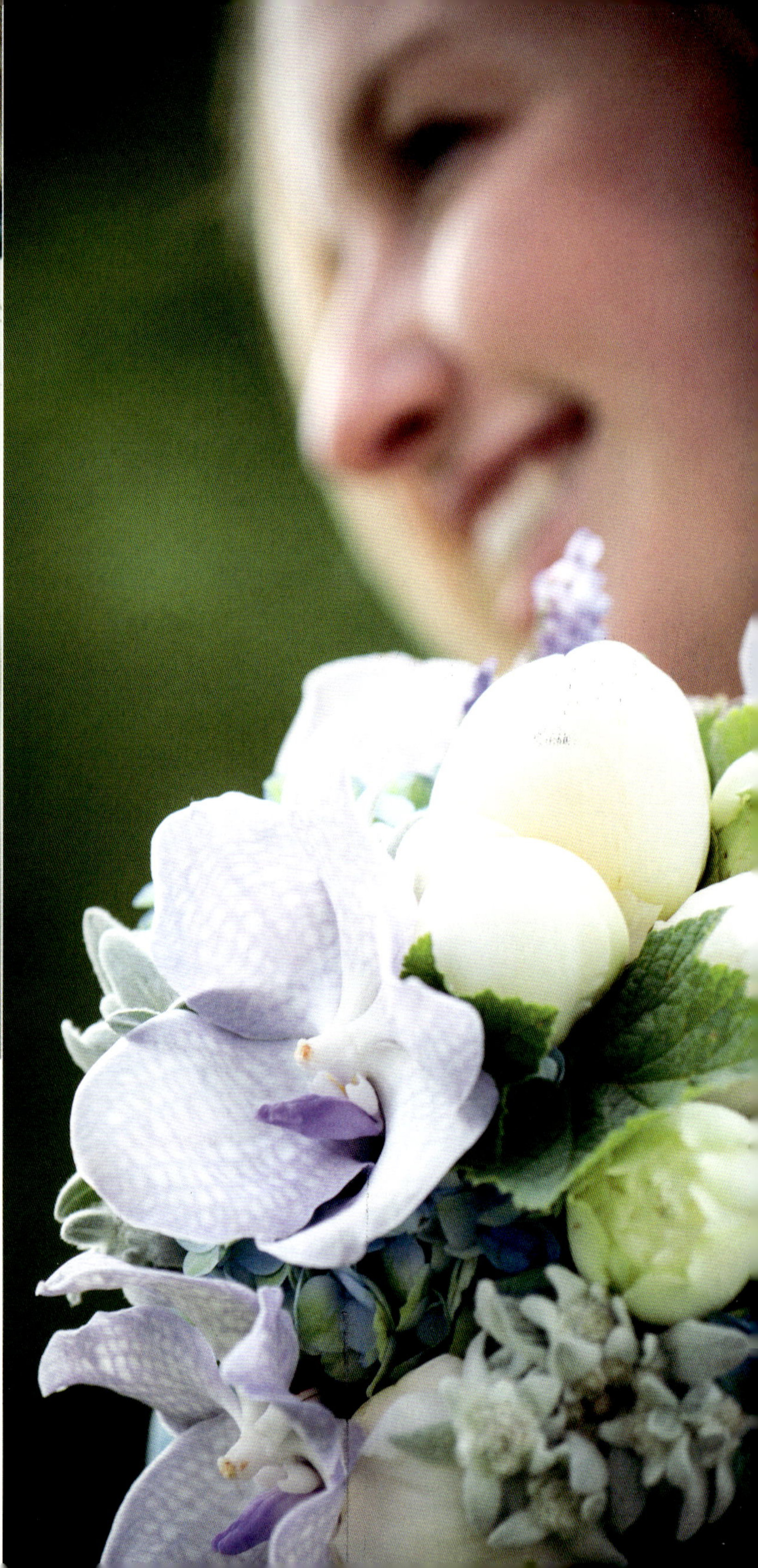

Hydrangea
Leontopodium alpinum
Paeonia 'Duchesse de Nemours'
Ribes tricolor
Rosa 'Blanchette'
Triticum
Vanda Kanchana® 'Lavender Mist'
Vicia cracca

Allium tuberosum
Aspidistra
Ranunculus
Vanda Tayanee® 'White'

Daphne sp.
Phalaenopsis 'Venice'

Ozothamnus
Phalaenopsis 'Venice'

Gloriosa rotschildiana
Heuchera
Rosa 'Piano'
Salix
Viburnum opulus

Gloriosa rotschildiana
Heuchera
Ribes rubrum
Rosa 'Piano'
Salix
Viburnum opulus

Aspidistra
Eucharis
Hydrangea
Ranunculus
Viburnum opulus

Delphinium

Hydrangea
Vanda Tayanee® 'Blue'
veneer

Dianthus 'Moon Aqua'
Lathyrus odoratus
Muscari
Vanda Sumathi® 'Dark Violet'

Aspidistra
Dianthus barbatus 'Green Trick'
Fritillaria
Iberis
Jasminum officinale
Ranunculus
Rosa 'Blanchette'
Rosa 'Green Eye'
Viburnum opulus

Rosa 'Green Tea'
Xanthorrhoea
veneer

Helleborus
Hydrangea
Scabiosa
Vanda Kanchana® 'Lavender Mist'
Viburnum opulus

Lathyrus latifolius
Rubus tricolor
Vanda Sundanda®
'Moonlight Blue'
Vanda Tayanee® 'Blue'
moneymaker

Ceropegia sandersonii
Cortina
Dianthus 'Country'
Vanda Tayanee® 'White'
Vanda Tayanee® 'Blue'

Anthriscus sylvestris
Chlorophytum comosum 'Bonnie'
Dianthus barbatus 'Green Trick'
Dianthus sp.
Hydrangea 'Emerald Green'
Lathyrus odoratus
Morus
Rosa 'Green Eye'
Rosa 'White Naomi'
Vanda Tayanee® 'White'
Viburnum opulus

Rosa 'Blanchette'
Vanda Tayanee® 'White'

Xerophyllum tenax
Zantedeschia 'Captain Venture'

Adiantum
Agapanthus
Anemone pulsatilla
Clematis
Hydrangea macrophylla 'Pimpernel'
Myosotis
Rosa 'Snowflake'
Rosa 'Green Eye'
bleached palm leaves

Zantedeschia 'Captain Venture'

Dendrobium nobile
Kalanchoë

Phalaenopsis 'Venice'
Protea

Special thanks to

118 - 119

My incomparable, dedicated team of photographers:
Kris Dimitriadis, I love the intensity and mutual appreciation in our way of
working together, always a pleasure to look back at so many beautiful and
unforgettable images.
Kurt Dekeyzer, thanks for the many years of fantastic teamwork and your
endless enthousiasm to continue this Flowers in Love series. I have fond
memories of days full of hard work and great laughs when creating
the best possible photographs.

Stichting Kunstboek, Katrien and Karel.
Visiting you feels a little like coming home. Thanks for the support
and creating the best conditions to make a beautiful book.

Assistants, thanks for your enthusiasm and dedication:
Hilde Viaene, Audrey Gatineau, Mélanie Lebris, Tiffany de Ham,
Alice Pedergnana, Elodie Choux, Anouk Putman, Trees De Buyssere,
Elise Choquel, Yukako Kameda

Ward, for always being there for me, for your technical ingenuity and for
supporting even my wildest plans.
Thanks for the many years of encouragment and your warm presence.

Family and friends:
I treasure your company, even though creativity and work often stand
in the way of meeting up with all of you. Thanks for being so understanding.

Models, thanks for your time, patience and positive attitude:
Lien d'Haeseleer, Valerie Oosterlinck, Céline De Vuyst, Mona Naudts,
Ann-Sophie Verhamme, Liesbeth Claeyssens, Tim en Nora Vijncke,
Elodie, Audrey en Tiffany

Christel Boone, for the stunning wedding dresses.

My students and passionate colleagues. In particular I'd like to thank:
Mark Pampling, Neill Strain, Geert Pattyn, Vadim Kazanskiy,
Hitomi Gilliam and Rudy Casati

Serax, Axel Vanden Bossche and Frank Lambert
Anco, Vanda orchids, Steef Van Adrichem
Familie Hemschoote, Rekad publishing, fleur creatief magazine
Smithers-Oasis, Chris Martens and Jan Joris
Lehner Wolle3, Felecitas Lehner and Sandra Mitter
Avalane, Wim Gyselen
PSG
An Theunynck
Hugo Hendriks
Dimitri Barbe
Luc and Marina Mortier
Kris Verbiest, Deb's Club
Rita De Vos
Philippe Poulain
Maria Vervynck-Dhont, Kurt Van De Veire, Kris Vanden Abeele
Ruth De Cooman
Hilde Van Cleemput and Michaël Borremans
Garage Autekie, Stefaan and Daisy
Petra Bruyneel, Protea iberica

The flower wholesalers for their impeccable service:
Agora, always a pleasure visiting you with special gratitude
for the Agora Special rose 'Moniek Vanden Berghe'
Euroflor: Monique, Robert, Ilse and Kristof, great business
with a familial feel
Bart De Rijcke, Dora Flora
Florist Center (Wevelgem)

Moniek Vanden Berghe

Training in floristry, IMOV, Ghent

Teacher Marc Derudder

Demonstrations and workshops in Belgium, the Netherlands, Germany, Scotland, UK, Ireland, France, USA, Japan, Australia, Finland, Mexico, Korea, Russia...

Kris Dimitriadis

Has been working at PSG since 2007, where he combines photography and graphic design. Gradually Kris specialized in the photography of floral design. He is passionate about his creative-expressive work and the new technical possibilities in his field of expertise.

Kurt Dekeyzer

Studied photography at the VZH in Hasselt (laureate).

Founder of Photo Studio Graphics (PSG), a full-service agency with a photo studio and design department. PSG Editions publishes a number of high-level magazines about lifestyle and architecture.

Creations / Créations / Creaties
Moniek Vanden Berghe
Eeksken 109
BE-9920 Lovendegem
T. + 32 477 68 52 77
www.cleome.be

Photography / Photographies / Fotografie
Photo Studio Graphics
Kurt Dekeyzer
Kris Dimitriadis
Kempische Steenweg 293 bus 26
BE-3500 Hasselt
T. +32 11 22 09 95
www.psg.be

Co-ordination / Coordination / Coördinatie
Karel Puype
Katrien Van Moerbeke

Texts / Textes / Tekst
Moniek Vanden Berghe
Geert Pattyn
Hitomi Gilliam
Mark Pampling
Neill Strain
Vadim Kazanskiy
Rudy Casati

Final editing / Rédaction finale / Eindredactie
Katrien Van Moerbeke

Translation / Traduction / Vertaling
Taal-Ad-Visie

Layout / Mise en pages / Vormgeving
www.groupvandamme.eu

Print / Impression / Druk
www.pureprint.be

Published by / Une édition de / Een uitgave van
Stichting Kunstboek bvba
Legeweg 165
B-8020 Oostkamp
T. +32 50 46 19 10
F. +32 50 46 19 18
info@stichtingkunstboek.com
www.stichtingkunstboek.com

ISBN 978-90-5856-500-6
D/2014/6407/19
NUR 421

Previously published

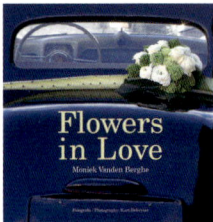

Flowers in Love
978-90-5856-161-9

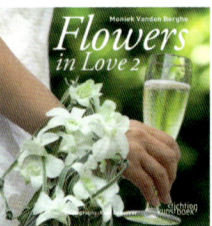

Flowers in Love 2
978-90-5856-224-1

Flowers in Love 3
978-90-5856-337-8

Flowers in Tears
978-90-5856-268-5

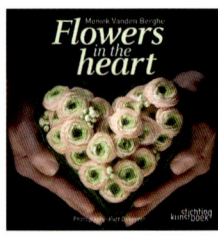

Flowers in the heart
978-90-5856-397-2

Moniek Vanden Berghe Monograph
978-90-5856-340-8